Setting Your Goals & Creating A Plan To Achieve Them

www.behindthescenechic.com

MELISSA AMBERS

Fast Track Guide: Setting Your Goals and Creating a Plan to Achieve Them

Goals without a plan to achieve them are just dreams. If you really want to achieve something, you need to learn how to set goals, create a realistic plan, and implement the plan. Time is the great equalizer. You must remember that everyone has the same 24 hours in a day in which to achieve their goals. When you make plans correctly, according to your goals, you will become a high achiever.

Know What You Want to Achieve

The very first part of setting any goal is to understand what it is that you want to achieve. Don't think of all the steps yet about getting to that goal, instead think about the goal itself and what it means. What is the big result of reaching the goal?

Define the Goal

Wanting to lose weight, write a book, or keep a clean house are all examples of goals but they aren't really what you achieve. When you lose weight, you achieve better health, a nicer physique, and more self-confidence. These are better ways to describe what you want to achieve. What is the result of the action? When you finish the book, lose the weight, finish that course – what now?

Let Go of Limiting Ideas

To identify what you want to achieve you may need to do some work on your limiting ideas and beliefs. Everyone has some. If you have an "I can't" mindset, you'll need to work on it so that you can make big goals for yourself. Can't messages consist of internal dialogue in your head that stops you from truly achieving anything big.

Identify Can't Messages

Try to identify any of the "can't messages" you're holding onto as you write down your goals that you want to achieve. If you want a 10K square foot house in the mountains but, as you do it, your mind is telling you that you can't, you really can't. Your mind is always right. You must switch on your "can do" attitude by being realistic with the plan of action to achieve your goals.

Great examples of limiting beliefs are thinking you're too old, too young, not skilled enough, or you don't have enough money to get started. These beliefs aren't true because they can be overcome or adjusted. Think about all the new technology that has enabled new businesses to start like Uber and Lyft. Uber and Lyft had a lot of laws and regulations that inhibited starting the business. However, instead of stopping they found a way to change the laws. They didn't let the law stand in their way and limit their goals.

Know Why You Want To Achieve It

In addition, it's imperative that you know why you're doing it. Why do you want to achieve that goal in the first place? Maybe you have set a goal to learn something new for your job such as learning new software. What is the reason you want to learn it? Do you want to learn how to use the new software because your boss made you, or if you're your own boss, is it because it's going to make your workflow smoother? What are the reasons for wanting to achieve that goal?

Your Why is Your Motivation

Knowing why something is important to you will help motivate you more than just knowing what you want to achieve. If you'll get a promotion, the software will help you gain more clients, or the software will help you make money, those are all reasons why you want to achieve the goal.

But, if you have no reason for doing it, you may just be wasting time. This is sometimes called "bright shiny object syndrome." If your answer is because someone else is doing it, or you have no idea why you're doing it, it's not the right goal for you to pursue.

This is the one time you should be selfish in your assessment. Maybe you genuinely don't want to do what you thought you did. But, often, not wanting to do something but dreaming of doing something signifies a problem with scarcity thinking. Dreamers have limiting beliefs that impede their goal achievements. Doers don't.

Analyze your goals and write down why you want to do them. Think about how you will feel once you have accomplished the goal. Will you feel good about it? Usually, if you know exactly why you want to do something, and the reason is something positive your motivation to accomplish it will increase exponentially.

Understand SMART Goal Setting

There is something called SMART goal setting. The letters stand for something different depending on who is explaining it but in general, SMART Goals are specific, measurable, achievable, realistic, and timely.

So instead of saying, "I want to lose weight" or even "I want to lose 30 pounds" it's imperative that you are very specific.

"I want to lose 30 pounds in 40 weeks from Monday. I will do this by counting my calories, eating an average of 1800 calories a day of low-carb, whole foods, plus walking at least 15K steps, 5 days per week which I will measure on my Fitbit."

Immediately, you can see that this goal is very specific, measurable, achievable, realistic, and timely. It can help to write out the acronym and then write a sentence regarding your goal that matches each part of the acronym so that you don't forget any aspect that will make your goal more achievable in the long run.

This is what a SMART goal would look like for this guide.

S – Write 3500 to 4000 words report about goal setting and planning by the 10th of the month.

M – 3500 to 4000 words (you can measure by word count)

A – Am I knowledgeable about the topic? Yes. Can I research the topic? Yes (it is attainable)

R – Do I have time to do this by the due date? Is this a realistic timetable?

T – Is there a deadline for completion? Yes.

Once create a SMART goal, you can break down the actions needed to complete and achieve your goal.

Chunk it Up & Break it Down

Once you write down your goal it's time to plan. When you look at an overall goal, it can seem very intimidating. Losing 30 pounds seems daunting but if you break that down into five-pound increments, it won't seem as daunting.

If you need to write an 80,000-word book, don't think about those 80K words. Instead, chunk things up to create one step for each part such as "Write a synopsis about the book." Or "Write an outline for Chapter One." Work your way through each part chunking it up and breaking it down into small pieces that can be accomplished in one work session.

Example: Chunk it up and break it down by looking at the various parts. 4000 words will take about 3 hours to write. (Note: Your timeline needs to be realistic for you, it might take you more or less time, and there is no right or wrong time limit, as long as it's realistic and fits your schedule and ability.) How much time do I have to do it? Let's say we're going to take 4 days to do it.

So, we chunk it down to this:

Day 1: Research 1 hour

Day 2: Write Outline 1 hour

Day 3: Write Content 3 hours

Day 4: Edit 1 hour

By looking at the chunks you can see that you need to have a big block of time available for day three, but if you have more time until the due date you could even break day three down into several days if you needed to.

For example, if your outline had five sections you could choose to work on one section per day. The point is to chunk it down in a realistic way that enables you to produce your best work. Chunking only works when you're very specific about your time. Don't overestimate how much time you can do anything it's better to underestimate so that you really will be able to stick to your schedule.

Some people do well just make a list, others need extra help such as with a mind map to organize all the different components of their goal. Yet others like to make flow charts. It's up to you and depends on how your mind works.

For some people, the best way to chunk up a project is to think in terms of what needs to be done rather than when. You can go back later and add in timelines based on your calendar. Just write a chronological list of what needs to happen to see the project through to completion and analyze the time requirements later.

The best way for most people is to start with the end in mind and work backward to today, based on the time constraints you have. Doing this is helpful for other reasons too. As you break everything down you can also note the different supplies, equipment, or information you'll need to achieve each chunk of the goal. Once you make your plan, keep your eyes firmly on each chunk. Avoid looking at the results until you're done.

Schedule Everything into Your Calendar

A very important part of making plans that achieve results is to be super realistic about how much time you really have. If you're working on a novel, don't think that you'll be able to do it all in a week. Thinking about the result at this point is too overwhelming. Now that you've chunked everything down, look at your list and determine how long each part will take you. Be realistic. Look at your lifestyle. Get out a calendar and fill in the things you already do.

First Things First

First, fill in your calendar with all the things you already normally do. Don't forget to include eating, bathing, shopping, time with your family and activities with friends. Even include your morning cup of coffee on the terrace. Leave nothing out. If you have a baby, it's likely you may only be able to do the work you want to do when someone else is watching them, or they're asleep. If you have a day job and you want to write the next Great Novel, then you will need to be realistic about that time factor.

Be Realistic about Time & Specific About What

When you've filled in the calendar, you can see how much available time you have to work on your goal. If you realize you, only have two hours a day, that's okay. Schedule those two hours a day in a very specific way.

Don't just put in the schedule "writing," "exercising", "or whatever" put in the schedule exactly what you're doing during that time frame.

For example, "Write a synopsis of chapter 1" or "Write an outline of Chapter one" be specific about what you're going to get done in that two hours. This one thing is truly the key to success because when you know exactly what you need to do during the time limit, you're more likely to get it done. Keep in mind how long it takes you do realistically do things. You're not going to write 20K words in 2 hours. Realistically you may be able to write less than 1000.

This is also true for exercise. "Walk five miles" as a goal for someone might take shorter or longer for different people depending upon their health and athletic ability. You might be able to walk a mile in 15 minutes while someone else takes 20. Creating an accurate schedule might take some trial and error to perfect but once you do, you'll start feeling as if you have more time than you did before. But remember, everyone has the same 24-hour days, so you don't have more time. You just do a better job of scheduling your time.

Tip: Google Calendar is free, and you can typically use it with any type of mobile device. You can also set alarms to remind you when to stop or start something. It's important to stick to your schedule. Alarms can help you stay on track.

Don't Wait for Inspiration

One reason that people end up running out of time to do things is that they tend to wait until they feel inspired. But that's backward thinking. Inspiration comes from doing. So, when your calendar tells you to do whatever it is that you've scheduled do it. As you're doing it, you're going to gain inspiration. The more times you stick to your schedule the more inspiration you're going to develop.

Habits & Rituals Beat Inspiration Every Time

The best thing you can do for yourself is to develop habits and rituals that will help you produce results and ultimately achieve your goals. Figure out what time of day is best for you to do whatever it is that you plan to do and then make it sacred. Let it become a habit and you'll soon be a high achiever. People will wonder how you ever get so much done. But, you do it because you've set your schedule and you stick to it with very few exceptions. If the house isn't on fire, keep going.

If you ask most any high achiever how they get things done they'll tell you it's due to their schedule. That's why your calendar is so important. Even Maya Angelou would rent a hotel room to write and write during specific hours. She didn't even sleep there but that's how she maintained a ritual and created a habit that got things done. When you do that, you don't need inspiration or motivation.

Once something has become a habit, it's hard to break that habit. Habits can be good or bad. In By avoiding the need for inspiration or motivation and sticking to a schedule, you can develop a positive habit. It works for anything. Let's say your house is messy and you want a cleaner house. Instead of saying, "I will clean my house" chunk things down, schedule them, and make them habits.

When you come home, instead of tossing your stuff on the nearest surface, have a home for everything and put it up immediately. Instead of mopping whenever you feel like it, mop directly after messes are made and then on specific days and times, you set up in your calendar. Eventually, it'll seem as if they house is on automatic.

If you want to stop snacking, don't buy snacks. A lot of things seem super simple and they are if you create habits and ritualize the things you want to accomplish.

Get Rid of Distractions

Today's world is full of distractions. Social media, games, friends, family, work, shopping, eating, sleeping – we all have so much to get done and we have so many interruptions. The fact is people cannot multitask. There are people who think that they're good multitaskers, but scientific evidence suggests that it's all bogus. No one can multitask and in fact trying to do that tends to lower your productivity, kill motivation, and make us feel as if we're never able to enjoy our life and are always working.

The calendar can help a lot. But you must stop multitasking as well as get rid of distractions. When you do, you'll discover that you can work so much faster than you thought possible and that you feel like you're living your life instead of watching it unfold. You should understand and truly get it that multitasking doesn't work for most people. Studies do not support the idea that anyone is good at

<u>multitasking</u>. You're not going to be the one who is good at multitasking, statistically speaking.

The best way to test this theory out for yourself is to start focusing on one thing at a time. If you're with your family, be with your family 100 percent. If you're at work, be at work, 100 percent. If you're working on a project, turn off the internet, the music, and the TV and just work on the project. If you want to play around on social media, that's fine, set up a time to do it in your calendar. Just don't fool yourself into thinking that you're going to be the exception to the rule and be an awesome multitasker. If you tend to multitask, you're not living up to your full potential.

In fact, most people are so bad at multitasking you should run from anyone who claims to be good at it. You should, in fact, reject the idea completely so that you can become a high achiever by setting goals, making concrete plans, and then accomplishing them by focusing on the plans exclusively.

Persevere

The thing that separates achievers from everyone else is that they keep going. They persevere. They continue to stick to what they were doing over the long term. They don't diet for three days and then give up. They stick to it. They make the right plans. They schedule everything in a realistic manner and then they follow the plan.

Novel writers don't write whenever the "mood" strikes. They write during bad days and good days, until they are finished. If someone is training for a marathon, they stick to the training every-single-day. If you want to set goals and truly achieve those goals, this is something that you must develop.

Michael Chabon, a Pulitzer Prize-winning writer has a schedule that he sticks to no matter what. He writes five nights per week from 10 PM to 3 AM. He doesn't deviate from that when he's working on a piece. This idea can work for any type of project. Small things lead to big results, in the end. A great book to read about this idea is The Compound Effect by Darren Hardy. You can use these methods to accomplish literally any goal that you want.

It's important to identify any blockers that are getting in your way to sticking to your plans. For example, if you have set a goal to lose weight and part of that involves going to the gym but you find that you're just not sticking to your schedule you may need to figure out why. Is the time you picked unrealistic? At what moment are you giving yourself permission to go off plan? When you can identify that, change it, and then move forward you'll start being able to stick to your plans better and longer.

Getting Started

Setting your goals and creating a plan to achieve them requires some understanding of goal setting, planning, and implementing. As you work toward improving your skills in these areas, you'll soon feel as if you have more hours in your day, more time for leisure activities, and feel more satisfied with your life because you're getting things done with purpose instead of waiting for that elusive inspiration and motivation to appear.

To begin, determine your goals, write them down the SMART way, and know why you want to do them so that you will feel motivated. Then, chunk them down into steps without concern about time. Just write a long chronological list (or you can use a mind map) to determine all the steps necessary to complete the goal.

Once you do that, insert the times and dates into your calendar with specifics about what you'll do during that time and date. Get rid of any distractions that might impede your chances of doing a good job. Avoid multitasking and focus 100 percent on each thing you put in your calendar that you want and need to do. You'll find that you become faster and more well-rounded as you do this. Finally, stick to it. Don't give up. Sometimes you may have to tweak your schedule to be more realistic but as you focus on your goals, planning, and action, you'll get better at it. No goal will be too hard for you to accomplish when you know what it takes to achieve it and set a plan in motion to do so. What are you waiting for?

Setting Goals & Achieving Them - Worksheet

Name: ____

Goal: ____

Due Date: ____

To Reach Goal I Need to Do: (list in order)

____

____

____

____

____

____

I Will Reach My Goal Because (your why)

____

____

____

____

____

What Does the Goal Achieved Look Like?

What Methods Will I Use to Stick to My Goal?

What Calendar System Will I Use to Stick to My Goals?

____

____

____

____

____

____

____

Define Distractions You'll Avoid

____

____

____

____

____

Make Your Goals SMART.

Specific

Measurable

Achievable

Realistic

Timely

WRITE SPECIFIC GOALS

I will _______________________________________

by/in _______________________________________

using/with ___________________________________

to reach my goal.

Ex: I will lose 40 lbs., in 50 weeks using a diet consisting of 1800 calories per day of whole foods and exercising by walking 10K steps 5 days per week to reach my goal.

ADDITIONAL THOUGHTS

NOTES

NOTES

NOTES

NOTES

NOTES

NOTES

NOTES